CANADIAN WRITERS AND THEIR WORKS

Cumulated Index, Fiction Series

CANADIAN WRITERS AND THEIR WORKS

Cumulated Index, Fiction Series

Edited by Donald W. McLeod

ECW PRESS, 1993

CANADIAN CATALOGUING IN PUBLICATION DATA

Main entry under title;
  Canadian writers and their works cumulated index : fiction series

Supplement to: Canadian writers and their works : fiction series.
ISBN 1-55022-142-6

1. Canadian writers and their works : fiction series – Indexes.   2. Canadian fiction (English) – History and criticism – Indexes.*   3. Authors, Canadian (English) – Biography – Indexes.*
I. McLeod, Donald W. (Donald Wilfred), 1957–

PS8187.C32 1993   016.813'009   C91-095093-8
PR9192.2.C32   1993   74787

Copyright © ECW PRESS, 1993

Design and imaging by ECW Type & Art, Oakville, Ontario.
Printed and bound by Hignell Printing Limited, Winnipeg, Manitoba.

Distributed by General Publishing Co. Limited, 30 Lesmill Road, Don Mills, Ontario M3B 2T6.

Published by ECW PRESS, 1980 Queen St. E., Toronto, Ontario M4L 1J2.

PREFACE

THE IDEA FOR THE *Canadian Writers and Their Works* series was first put forward in 1980. It was a big, original plan — nothing less than to produce an authoritative, well-researched, and well-documented critical series covering the development of Canadian writing over the past two centuries. Other critical reference books on Canadian literature had already appeared, but there was nothing of this depth or magnitude. From its inception, *Canadian Writers and Their Works* was envisioned as a bold new approach to the study of Canadian writing.

The project editors assembled a team of Canadian literary specialists to write individual essays on Canadian writers. Each specialist devoted an essay to *one* particular author. In addition, much time was spent in editing and updating the essays and in performing independent verification of facts and sources. This attention to detail necessitated publishing the series over a period of years — almost ten years elapsed between the appearance of the first volume, in 1983, and the publication of the final volumes, in 1992. The result is that *Canadian Writers and Their Works* is the most comprehensive and accurate commentary to date; it also includes a wealth of previously unknown information about individual Canadian writers.

The essays have been combined in twenty volumes that are arranged chronologically to present Canada's literary history as it has evolved over the last two centuries. Ten of these volumes are devoted to writers of fiction, and ten to poets. Each volume, in turn, contains four or five essays that are unified in a general introduction by George Woodcock. Each critical essay includes a brief biography of the author, a discussion of the tradition/milieu influencing his/her work, a critical overview section that reviews published criticism of the author, a long section analyzing the author's works, and a selected

5

bibliography listing primary and secondary material. Each essay includes an original illustration of the writer by Isaac Bickerstaff, and each volume is fully indexed.

The project editors of *Canadian Writers and Their Works* wish to acknowledge the contributions of the many people who have played an important role in creating this series. First, we would like to thank the critics who prepared the essays for these volumes (complete listing on pages 8–10), as well as George Woodcock, for his incisive Introductions to each volume. Don Evans (a.k.a. Isaac Bickerstaff) drew the marvelous illustrations of the authors. We are indebted to the following people for their editorial and verification work: Edna Barker, Matthew Carnicelli, Graham Carr, Val Daigen, Jamie Gaetz, Bob Hilderley, Jeff Jones, Ken Lewis, Ross MacKay, Don McLeod, Scott Mitchell, Nanette Norris, Tom Orman, Holly Potter, Carole Turner, Anne Williams, Mary Williams, and Jean Wilson. We are also pleased to acknowledge the production and design teams of Paul Davies of ECW Type & Art and Tim and Elke Inkster of The Porcupine's Quill, and the keyboarding skills of Debra Burke, Pat Kenny, Wiesia Kolasinska, Stephanie Termeer, Jennifer Trainor, and Hilda Keskin Weber. Special thanks to Tom Orman for his help in keying the cumulated indexes.

Robert Lecker/Jack David/Ellen Quigley
Project Editors
Canadian Writers and Their Works

A NOTE ABOUT
THE CUMULATED INDEX

THE PRESENT VOLUME is an edited, slightly revised cumulation of the indexes that appeared with each of the *Canadian Writers and Their Works* volumes. This index lists all proper names mentioned in the volumes, excluding place names, academic institutions, names of characters, and names of relatives mentioned only in passing. All critics named or quoted in the text or in explanatory notes are indexed. All titles of poems, stories, articles, books, etc., that are discussed in the text are indexed, as are the titles of periodicals and critical works about which substantive remarks have been made.

The index is arranged alphabetically, word by word, and chronologically if there are separate entries for different editions of the same work. Names beginning with McC are indexed as McC, not Mac. Abbreviations such as St., No., and Mrs. are indexed as they are spelled, not as if spelled out in full. Where titles are identical or are similar to works by other writers, the author's last name is also listed, in parenthesis. Pseudonymous names are listed under the pseudonym (e.g., Twain, Mark), with the person's real name listed in parenthesis afterwards (Samuel L. Clemens). Newspapers are indexed by city, and the titles of college publications cite the name of the school in parenthesis. Continuous pagination (e.g., 47–49) is cited only if the discussion of the topic is also continuous.

LIST OF CONTENTS: FICTION SERIES

*Each volume contains a critical
introduction by George Woodcock.*

Volume I:

Frances Brooke by Lorraine McMullen
Susanna Moodie by Michael Peterman
John Richardson by Dennis Duffy
Catharine Parr Traill by Carl Ballstadt
Three Writers of Victorian Canada (Rosanna Leprohon,
     James De Mille, Agnes Maule Machar) by Carole Gerson

Volume II:

Thomas Chandler Haliburton by Stan McMullin
William Kirby by Margot Northey
Gilbert Parker by Elizabeth Waterston
Charles G.D. Roberts by Terry Whalen
Ernest Thompson Seton by Lorraine McMullen

Volume III:

Ralph Connor by John Lennox
Sara Jeannette Duncan by Thomas Tausky
Stephen Leacock by Ralph Curry
Robert Stead by Eric Thompson

Volume IV:

Frederick Philip Grove by W.J. Keith
Raymond Knister by Joy Kuropatwa
W.O. Mitchell by Dick Harrison
Martha Ostenso by Stan Atherton
Sinclair Ross by Morton Ross

Volume X:

Leonard Cohen by Linda Hutcheon
Dave Godfrey by Michael Larsen
Robert Harlow by Louis MacKendrick
Jack Hodgins by David Jeffrey
Robert Kroetsch by Peter Thomas

Cumulated Index to
Canadian Writers and Their Works,
Fiction Series, Volumes 1–10